Language: English

These materials are designed to assist you in learning about hope. They should not be used for medical advice, counseling, or other health-related services. iFred, The Shine Hope Company and Kathryn Goetzke do not endorse or provide any medical advice, diagnosis, or treatment. The information provided herein should not be used for the diagnosis or treatment of any medical condition and cannot be substituted for the advice of physicians, licensed professionals, or therapists who are familiar with your specific situation. Consult a licensed medical professional, or call 911, if you are in need of immediate assistance.

ISBN: 978-1-954531-28-4

TABLE OF CONTENTS

RESOURCES/DISCLAIMER

As with any skill-building, developing Hope can be challenging. While working through this course, individuals may experience strong or unpleasant emotions, especially when reflecting on difficult situations or experiences of hopelessness. It's important to pay attention to your emotional responses. If you notice intense emotions, we recommend accessing additional resources for support. Below are some resources that may offer further assistance.

If you are in crisis, you can **text HOME to 741741** for immediate assistance.

For more resources, visit:
www.theshinehopecompany.com/recovery-resources/

Check out these episodes of The Hope Matrix podcast to learn how others have overcome challenges such as traumatic brain injury, grief, and homelessness.

- **Episode 19: From Heroin Addiction and Homelessness to Hope, featuring Grant Denton of The Karma Box Project** - *www.thehopematrix.com/2022/02/02/from-heroin-addiction-and-homelessness-to-Hope-featuring-grant-denton-of-the-karma-box-project/*

- **Episode 50: Living Authentically: A Journey through Challenges to Shine Hope, Featuring Lawanda Jackson** - *www.thehopematrix.com/episodes/living-authentically-a-journey-through-challenges-to-shine-hope-featuring-lawanda-jackson/*

PRE-LESSON: FINDING YOUR WHY

Recovery is a process, not a straight line. On average, individuals working toward recovery may experience relapse five times during serious efforts—and that's okay. Relapse is not a failure. It's a part of the journey, a moment to learn, adjust, and continue forward with greater strength and insight.

This workbook is designed to guide you in building and sustaining hope as a practical strategy for recovery. Through these modules, you'll learn how to set meaningful goals, maintain a positive mindset, and develop tools to manage stress all through the framework of growing hope.

You are not alone in this process. Hope is learnable, and it can be your greatest asset on the road to recovery.

Creating any new habit takes effort, commitment, and patience. It's not always easy, but with consistent practice and a clear understanding of why it matters to you, growth becomes possible—even in the face of challenges.

Think about this: If you were asked to run a mile today, how would that feel? Could you do it? Now, imagine running a mile every single day. Over time, it would likely become easier, and eventually, it might even feel natural.

That's what we Hope to achieve with learning Hope. We want the skills of Hope to become a part of your daily life—something that feels natural and automatic. Learning anything new can feel overwhelming at first, so before we dive in, take a moment to reflect on what's motivating you to be here.

What is your 'why' for participating in this Hope course? Why do you want to do the work? What motivates you to show up and engage with the materials? Why do you care about growing Hope? What is your 'why'?

_____

_____

_____

_____

Now that you have your initial why, let's dig deeper. Oftentimes, the true "why" that is linked to our values comes when we think a little deeper about why we are participating in certain work.

What is your why to your above answer?

_____

_____

What is your why to your above answer?

_____

_____

What is your why to your above answer?

_____

_____

Is that your final WHY? If not, what is your why to your above answer?

_____

_____

When things get hard, it is important to come back to your final why. This is WHY you are doing this work to learn the skill of Hope. This is why the work is important. Your why needs to anchor you in challenging times. Ask yourself the "why" question in relation to everything you need to be anchored in in your life; your family, spirituality, recovery, work, health, life, etc. Anchoring your WHY can keep you strong in times of struggles.

When challenges arise, what will help you stay committed to this learning?

_____

_____

CONNECTING HOPE TO YOUR RECOVERY JOURNEY

What are some of the reasons you decided to begin your recovery journey?

_____

_____

_____

_____

How does your recovery support you in creating the life you Hope for?

_____

_____

_____

_____

How does your recovery benefit those around you?

_____

_____

_____

_____

What are the steps you will take to incorporate Hope on your recovery journey?

_____

_____

_____

_____

What needs to happen for you to feel confident in continuing or beginning your recovery journey?

_____

_____

_____

_____

Keep these reflections close. Research shows that people are much more likely to achieve a goal when they write it down. By taking the time to reflect and write today, you've already taken an important step toward making Hope a lasting part of your life.

MODULE 1:

INTRODUCTION TO HOPE SCIENCE AND **SHINE HOPE™**

MODULE 1: INTRODUCTION TO HOPE SCIENCE AND **SHINE HOPE™**

INTRODUCTION TO HOPE

Thank you for choosing Hope

This is the first step on your Hope journey. Hope is a teachable, measurable, and learnable skill that has positive ramifications on every aspect of your life. Higher Hope is associated with greater emotional and psychological well-being, economic security, improved academic performance, less violence, less loneliness, and enhanced personal relationships, yet we are never taught about Hope or how to activate Hope in our lives.

We often think of Hope as a "wish," but Hope is so much more than that. We define Hope as a vision for something in your future, fueled by both positive feelings and inspired actions. Both feelings and actions are critical to Hope; actions are what differentiate Hope from a "wish."

There are many definitions for Hope, so we will discuss a few:

- **Dr. Shane Lopez, a Hope expert:** "Hope is the feeling you have when you have a goal, are excited about achieving that goal, and then you figure out how you can achieve your goal."
- **Dr. Dan Tomasulo, author of Learned Hopefulness:** "Hope is a reorganization of perceptions to foster the belief that you have control in the future."
- **Dr. Crystal Bryce, Associate Dean at the University of Texas at Tyler:** "Hope to me isn't squishy. Hope is something that we have control over. It is something cognitive. It's a skill. It's something that we can work toward."
- **Dr. Chan Hellman, Founding Director of the Hope Research Center:** "Hope is the belief that the future will be better than today."

To define Hope, our Founder, Kathryn Goetzke, started by looking at the definition of Hopelessness and worked her way toward defining Hope because ultimately, she wanted to figure out how we get from hopelessness to Hope. She created 'The Hope Matrix' and we use this definition for Hope:

HOPE is a vision for something in your future, fueled by both POSITIVE FEELINGS and INSPIRED ACTIONS.

Specifically relevant to populations in recovery, higher Hope is associated with

- Increased life satisfaction
- Decreased anxiety and depression.
- Decreased risk of homelessness
- Decreased risk of poverty
- Increased self-efficacy

Additionally, and most importantly, Hope is linked to the prevention of suicidal ideation and suicide attempts.

We created a simple image called The Hope Matrix™ to help everyone easily understand this construct. That way, no matter what challenge a person faces, they can look at The Hope Matrix and ask 'How can I best manage the Despair around this challenge and get back to Positive Feelings' and 'How can I move from Helplessness to Inspired Actions'. (See visuals on the next page)

If you have Hope, you must have both feelings and actions (otherwise all you have is a wish). Positive feelings are those feelings that help us to stay hopeful as we work toward our goals. Inspired Actions are the steps that propel us toward our goals. It is the cycle of positive feelings and Inspired Actions that create and sustain Hope.

We cannot make you hopeful. However, the lessons contained in this book can teach you the "how-to" of Hope, and give you the critical Hope skills to activate Hope in your life and the lives of those around you.

Your Hope journey is up to you. Similarly to learning any new skill, the more you use the skills outlined in this workbook, the easier it will be to use Hope in your life, increase your Hope level, and proactively manage hopelessness. And the more challenges you have in your life, the more you want to use Shine Hope skills.

Welcome to the Hopeful Mindsets community.

1 Grzesik & Ghosh (2023)

2 Gilman et al. (2012)

3 Duncan et al. (2022)

4 Begom (2023)

5 Saboor et al. (2019)

5 Luo et al. (2016)

THE
HOPE MATRIX™

POSITIVE FEELINGS

HIGH HOPE

The Five Keys to SHINE Hope™

- **S** TRESS SKILLS
- **H** APPINESS HABITS
- **I** NSPIRED ACTIONS
- **N** OURISHING NETWORKS
- **E** LIMINATE CHALLENGES

HELPLESSNESS

INSPIRED ACTIONS

HOPELESSNESS

DESPAIR

COMMON TERMS FOR HOPEFUL MINDSETS

The most important terms we use in this workbook, and that we Hope you begin to use in your daily life, include:

HOPE: We define Hope as a vision for something in the future, fueled by both positive feelings and inspired actions.

HOPELESSNESS: Hopelessness is both a feeling of despair and a sense of helplessness. It is emotional (a negative feeling) and motivational (an inability to act). We all experience moments of hopelessness and manage them with Hope skills.

POSITIVE FEELINGS: Positive feelings are those feelings that help us to stay Hopeful as we work toward our goals.

INSPIRED ACTIONS: Inspired actions are the deliberate steps you take to get in your upstairs brains and toward your goals in life.

UPSTAIRS BRAIN: This is where our thinking, imagining, problem-solving, and learning occur. This part of the brain is responsible for the development of sound decision-making and planning, control over emotions and body, and self-understanding and empathy. The upstairs brain is also where we access our positive feelings.

DOWNSTAIRS BRAIN: Also referred to as the reptilian brain, this part of the brain is responsible for basic functions such as breathing, blinking, heart rate, and fight, flight, freeze, or fawn mode. It is also responsible for the chemical stimulus associated with strong emotions, such as anger, sadness, and fear.

STRESS RESPONSE: Your stress response is when an external or internal trigger causes your brain to release stress hormones, such as cortisol, adrenaline, and norepinephrine, that force you into your fight, flight, freeze, or fawn mode. It generally lasts 90 seconds from the time of the last trigger.

STRESS SKILLS: These are actions that help you navigate your stress response and work through your body's chemical response to external stimuli to manage your downstairs brain and get you back upstairs.

HAPPINESS HABITS: These are healthy, long-term habits that help you stay in your upstairs brain, where you access the problem-solving skills, collaboration, and passion, all critical for Hope. When you take time for Happiness Habits, your brain releases happiness hormones, such as endorphins, dopamine, serotonin, and oxytocin.

NOURISHING NETWORKS: Your Nourishing Networks are the Hope Networks of the people in your life that provide you with support, help you stay on track, encourage you to succeed, and who you do the same for in return.

ELIMINATING CHALLENGES: Challenges to Hope are negative thinking patterns, like limiting beliefs, automatic negative thoughts, all-or-nothing thinking, negative bias, rumination, worry, focusing on uncontrollables, attaching to outcomes, and internalizing failure, that can keep us in hopelessness states. Eliminating challenges are the conscious act of using Hope skills to overcome these challenges and get back to Hope.

THE HOPE MATRIX™: The Hope Matrix is the process that we use to get from hopelessness to Hope. The Hope Matrix teaches us that to cultivate Hope, we must move from despair to positive feelings, and from helplessness to inspired actions.

Shine Hope™: This is the mnemonic we use to remember our Hope skills. Shine stands for: **S**tress Skills, **H**appiness Habits, **I**nspired Actions, **N**ourishing Networks, and **E**liminating Challenges and is what we use to activate skills for Hope.

THE HOPE MATRIX

The Hope Matrix is the process that we use to get from hopelessness to Hope. The Hope Matrix teaches us that to reach a hopeful mindset, we must move from despair to positive feelings, and from helplessness to inspired actions.

Directions: Fill in the blanks below with the following words: **Hope, Hopelessness, Despair, Helplessness, Positive Feelings, Inspired Actions.**

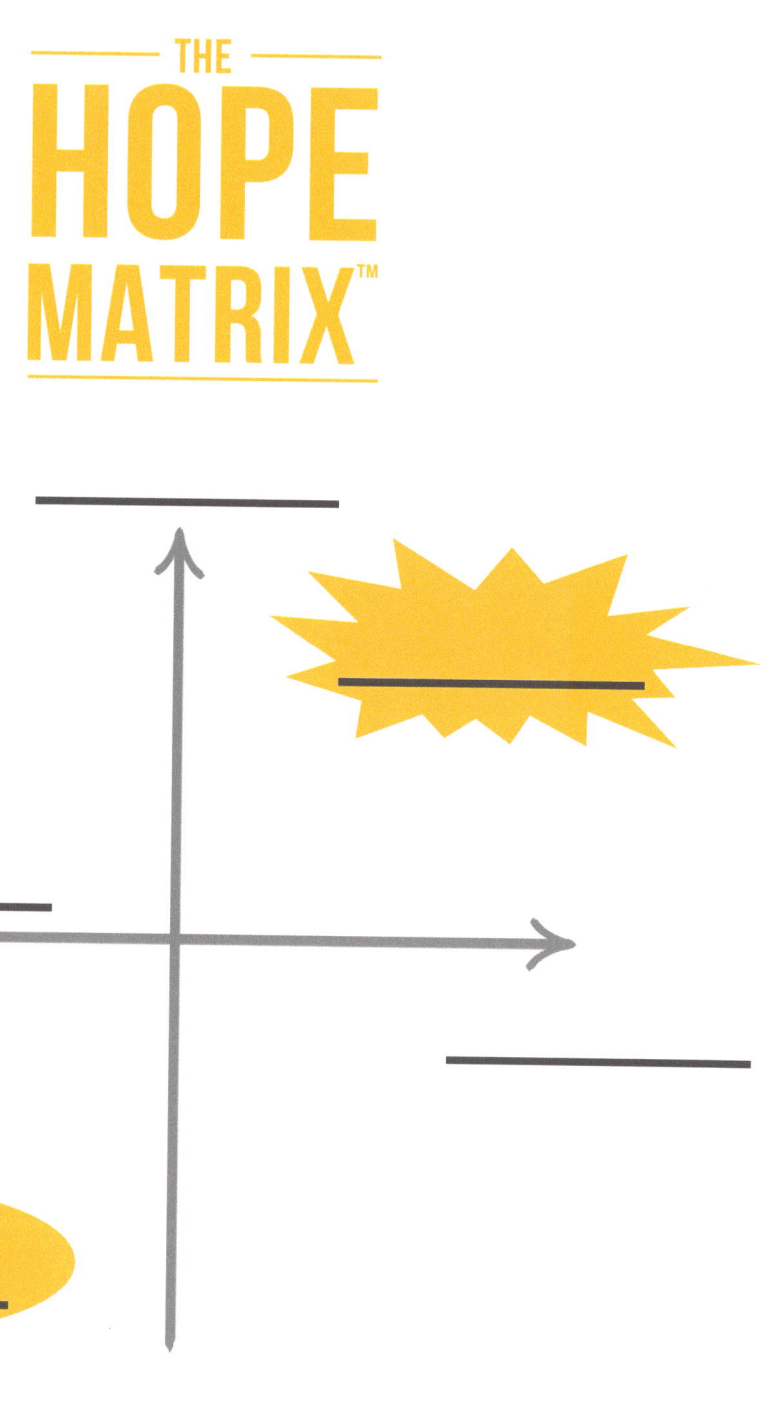

Answer keys on Page 36

HOPE SCALES

Your Hope score is a tool for you to use to monitor your progress, track your Hope journey, and reflect on how hopeful you are in the current moment. Hope is not fixed; when you practice Hope skills, you can improve your Hope score.

Use the link provided to take the Adult Snyder Hope Scale Assessment:

www.theshinehopecompany.com/measure-your-hope/

My Current Snyder Hope Scale Score: _____

Are there times in your life when you've experienced higher Hope? (Consider providing an example of a time you were most hopeful about something)

_____

_____

What was different in your life when you experience higher Hope?

_____

_____

How has your Hope impacted your ability to achieve goals?

_____

_____

How does Hope currently show up in your recovery journey?

_____

_____

How can Hope help you in your recovery journey?

_____

_____

What is preventing you from experiencing Hope?

_____

_____

What can help motivate you to practice Hope skills?

_____

_____

This course teaches you the Hope skills you can use to create, maintain, and grow Hope. There will be times throughout your life when you or someone you love experiences hopelessness. It is in these times, when your Hope score is at its lowest, that it is most important to practice skills to activate Hope.

The goal of this course is to learn the "how-to" of Hope so that you can both create a model for your own life and share the power of Hope with others.

Who in your life could benefit from higher Hope?

_____

_____

What organizations or businesses in your community could benefit from learning about Hope?

_____

_____

STRENGTHS FINDER

Understanding your strengths is important for creating and maintaining Hope. Focusing on your strengths can help you manage your stress response, cultivate positive thoughts, and focus on the future. As you continue through this workbook, you will repeatedly be asked to reflect on your strengths.

Take a moment to learn more about your strengths by taking the free VIA Character Strengths Survey here:

theshinehopecompany.pro.viasurvey.org

Write down the top five strengths you identify with:

1 _____   3 _____   5 _____

2 _____   4 _____

Which of these strengths do you think is most tied to your ability to maintain Hope?

_____

_____

Are you activating your strengths regularly? How so?

_____

_____

What does it look like when you use your strengths? (Provide an example of an activity that uses your strengths).

_____

_____

How can you better utilize your strengths at home? At work? In your recovery journey?

_____

_____

ANTITHESIS OF HOPE: HOPELESSNESS

MODULE 2: ANTITHESIS OF HOPE: HOPELESSNESS

What happens in the absence of Hope? Hopelessness. Many people talk about hopelessness, but do you really know what it is? When people say they are hopeless, what does that even mean? Most people think of hopelessness as a feeling of "despair." Yet that isn't the full story.

HOPELESSNESS is characterized by EMOTIONAL DESPAIR (e.g., sadness, anger, fear) and MOTIVATIONAL HELPLESSNESS (e.g., powerlessness and lack of action)[6]

This combination means that to address hopelessness, you need to focus on both feelings and *actions.*

Hopelessness is a normal response to hard things in life. It can be triggered by major life events, such as a death, or small obstacles, such as rush hour traffic. Hopelessness can also be caused by external factors such as discrimination, oppression, a global pandemic, or climate change. People who struggle with addiction may face hopelessness while they are deep in their addiction, as they begin their sobriety journey, during relapse, or throughout the recovery process. They may also experience hopelessness about relationship challenges and finances as they are working towards recovery.

No matter how big or how small the trigger is, hopelessness is overwhelming. It's therefore important that when we feel hopelessness, whatever the cause, we focus on moving from despair and helplessness back to positive feelings and inspired actions.

The thing about hopelessness, is you can manage it. You can always get from despair back to positive feelings, and always navigate from helplessness to inspired actions. It isn't always easy, yet it is always possible.

It is no surprise that hopelessness is associated with many negative life outcomes, including addictions, risky behaviors, violence, adverse health outcomes, and anxiety. Hopelessness is also a primary symptom of depression and a key predictor of suicide.

6 Abramsom et al. (1989)

In people who struggle with addiction, hopelessness is linked to:

- Decreased self-esteem
- Decreased treatment adherence
- Increased risk of violence
- Increased risk of suicidal ideation, depression, and anxiety

If we aren't proactive in our fight against hopelessness, it can lead to destructive behaviors, including substance use and misuse that cause harm to ourselves and the people around us.

Hopelessness is increasing in the United States and around the world. Learning the Hope skills in this course is so important, not only for us, but so that we can teach others. Hope is a teachable, learnable, measurable skill, that can help us identify and manage hopelessness. Not only can Hope help us move from despair and helplessness to positive feelings and Inspired Actions, it can help us empower others to do the same.

Many people recognize when they've had moments of hopelessness as times of emotional despair (sadness, anger, or fear). What do moments of emotional despair look like in your life? How do you manage sadness, anger, and fear?

_____

_____

_____

_____

When faced with moments of hopelessness, motivational helplessness is also an issue. How do you manage these feelings of powerlessness?

_____

_____

_____

_____

MY SHINE HOPE STORY™

Throughout this course, we'll explore the Five Keys to Shine Hope: Stress Skills, Happiness Habits, Inspired Actions, Nourishing Networks, and Eliminating Challenges. These keys offer pathways for transitioning from hopelessness to Hope. As we progress, you'll gain insight into how everyone manages feelings of hopelessness differently and finds their way back to Hope.

We use the Shine Hope framework more during moments of hopelessness. The following poster has clickable links so you can learn more about each of the skills we will discuss further throughout the group.

Moreover, to reinforce your understanding of these skills, you'll apply them to a real-life challenge you've encountered. Each module will introduce a new skill, prompting you to reflect on how you utilized it in the face of adversity or how you could have applied it to overcome the challenge.

To begin this journey, take some time to delve into one past challenge you've struggled with or a current challenge you are faced with. Think of something that has caused moments of hopelessness. Write about the challenge.

Applying the Shine framework to this past challenge will likely serve you well as you navigate challenges in the future. Describe the situation, your emotions, and what made it particularly challenging to overcome. This exercise will pave the way for a deeper understanding of how these Hope-building skills can be effectively utilized in various life scenarios.

Alternatively, if you do not want to write about yourself, choose a person (i.e., family member, friend, public figure, celebrity, etc.) who has had a similar challenge and use them as the person you will write about throughout the course.

MY SHINE HOPE STORY™

To add image in this area, edit the PDF via Adobe Acrobat or any PDF app editor.

MODULE 3:

STRESS SKILLS

STRESS SKILLS

The First Key to Shine Hope is identifying and managing your stress response using Stress Skills.[13]

It's important to understand the connection between your brain, body, and behavior so you can begin to use it to your advantage. When your mood changes, it may be so subtle that you don't pick up on it at first. However, your body does, and it reacts. These reactions are known as psychosomatic responses.

For example, when some people are triggered, they grind their teeth, their shoulders clench, and they sometimes even forget to breathe. All of these reactions are caused by the relationship between the brain and biology, which are connected by complex circuitry. They influence one another in various ways that can be hard to identify. Psychosomatic responses are manifestations of the state of your brain in your physical body, and can come in the form of discomfort, sensations, or habits.

Behaviors we engage in under stress are often the culmination of thoughts and feelings, and while this can sometimes seem problematic, such as when you snap at someone because you are stressed, it can also be incredibly beneficial, such as taking action during a time of crisis and saving someone's life. When you look at the connection between your brain, biology, and behavior through the lens of Hope, you can start to reframe how you think and feel.

Increasing Hope isn't just about influencing your brain; it is also about positively impacting your biology and behavior. When you positively impact your brain, you receive long-term benefits in multiple areas.

13 Sahranavard et al. (2018)

14 Mayo Clinic (2023)

15 Pace (2016)

As you continue your recovery journey, we invite you to gently explore how your body's response to stress may have shaped some of your past choices related to substance use. Reflecting on this connection can help you build greater awareness and compassion for yourself as you heal.

_____

_____

_____

_____

What are some ways your body lets you know when you're feeling stressed or unsafe?

_____

_____

_____

_____

Can you remember a time when stress or fear influenced a decision you made? What was happening in your body or mind at that time?

_____

_____

_____

_____

Looking back, were there moments when reacting to stress felt like the only option you had?

_____

_____

_____

_____

How did your environment or circumstances at the time affect how you responded to stress?

_____

_____

_____

_____

What coping strategies did you rely on when you felt overwhelmed? Did any of them help in the moment, even if they caused harm later on?

_____

_____

_____

_____

THE DOWNSTAIRS BRAIN. The downstairs brain, also known as the amygdala, includes the limbic region and brainstem[15]. It is the more primitive part of the brain (also referred to as the reptilian brain), and is responsible for basic functions such as breathing, blinking, heart rate, and fight, flight, or freeze mode. The downstairs brain is also responsible for the chemical stimulus associated with strong emotions, such as anger, rage, sadness, frustration, and fear.

THE UPSTAIRS BRAIN. Your upstairs brain is also known as the prefrontal cortex. It is where your thinking, imagining, learning, problem-solving, and creativity all occur. This part of your brain is responsible for the development of sound decision-making and planning, self-understanding, and empathy. The upstairs brain is also where you feel positive emotions, such as happiness, contentment, peace, and passion. You may remember that positive feelings are the first ingredient of Hope; this means that you can only access your Hope when you are in your upstairs brain.

It's important to remember that the downstairs brain is not a "bad" part of your brain. It is important for survival and it helps us understand the world around us. However, you don't want to be in your downstairs brain all the time. The Hope skills you are going to learn during this program will help you move from your downstairs brain into your upstairs brain so that you can always return to a Hopeful mindset.

MY BRAIN

Fill in the blanks with the emotions of the emoticon facial expressions that match using *fear,* *anger, sadness, relaxed, happy,* and *excited.*

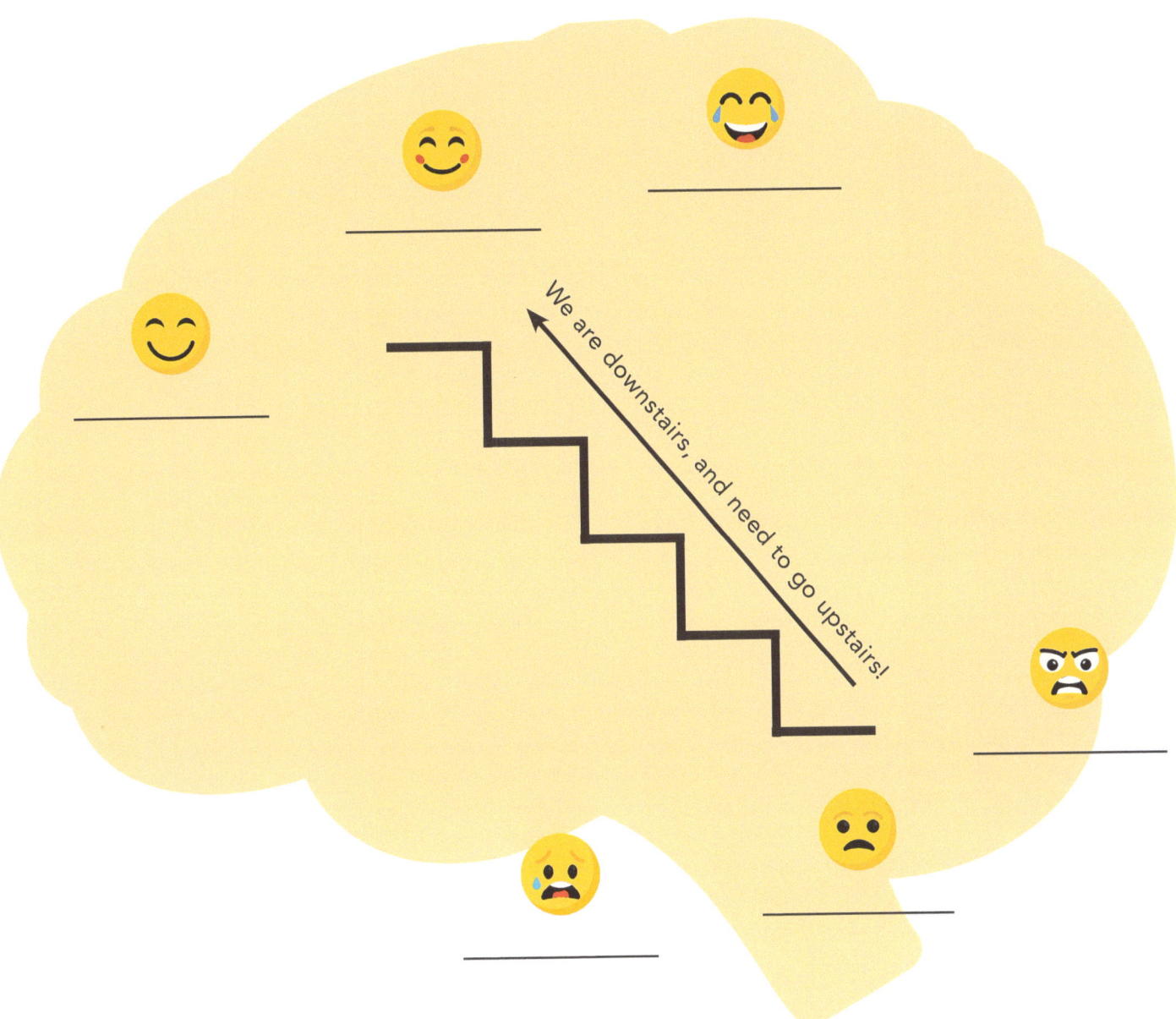

We are downstairs, and need to go upstairs!

Answer keys on Page 36

IDENTIFYING YOUR FEELINGS

The three main emotions associated with despair (the emotional component of hopelessness) are anger, fear, and sadness. When we are emotionally triggered, sadness, anger, and/or fear can activate our despair and cause us to move toward our downstairs brain.

However, we shouldn't simply push these emotions away, as that often leads to harmful behaviors, such as addiction, violence, and self-harm. It is important that when we feel despair, we proactively acknowledge the feeling, identify the root emotions that are causing the despair, and discover what they are telling us. Only once we have honored, experienced, explored, and learned from the emotion can we fully release it.

Using the questions below, think about the last time you experienced each of these emotions, and start to explore how you feel these emotions and express them.

ANGER

Describe the last time you were angry:

_____

How did you experience anger in your mind? _____

How did you experience anger in your body? _____

How did you respond when you were angry?

_____

What did your anger tell you about your environment or yourself?

_____

What are unhealthy ways you respond to anger? _____

What are healthy ways you respond to anger? _____

SADNESS

Describe the last time you were sad:

_____

How did you experience sadness in your mind? _____

How did you experience sadness in your body? _____

How did you respond when you were sad?

_____

What did your sadness tell you about your environment or yourself?

_____

What are unhealthy ways you respond to sadness? _____

What are healthy ways you respond to sadness? _____

FEAR

Describe the last time you were afraid:

_____

How did you experience fear in your mind? _____

How did you experience fear in your body? _____

How did you respond when you were afraid?

_____

What did your fear tell you about your environment or yourself?

_____

What are unhealthy ways you respond to fear? _____

What are healthy ways you respond to fear? _____

TRIGGER	LIMITING BELIEF	EMOTION FELT	WHERE IN MY BODY IS IT FELT	MY BEHAVIOR/ RESPONSE	STRESS SKILL I CAN USE	RESOLUTION TO TRIGGER EVENT
EXAMPLES Did poorly on quiz	I am a failure	Fear, shame	Stomach	Shut down, lose motivation to try	Deep breathing	I created a plan to stay on top of my coursework

STRESS RESPONSE

Dr. Jill Bolte Taylor developed the 90-second rule in her book, "My Stroke of Insight," to explain the biology behind your stress response. The 90-second rule says that a chemical process takes place in your body for approximately 90 seconds when you are triggered by something in your environment. For 90 seconds after the environmental trigger, your body is flooded with stress hormones, such as cortisol, adrenaline, and norepinephrine.

When you experience your stress response, you are in your downstairs brain, and can't reach your upstairs brain; the upstairs brain is the place where you make good decisions for moving toward all you Hope for in life.

Your ability to learn to proactively control this response is the First Key to Shine Hope because it is what empowers you to start controlling how you react to triggers in your environment. Are you controlling triggers, or are your triggers and other people controlling you?

You give others power over you every time you react to something someone else does or allow someone to "trigger" you. If they are trying to get a negative reaction from you and they succeed, you ultimately lose. When you learn to control your triggers and reactions, you can move into and remain in the upstairs brain.

You can manage your stress response using Stress Skills. By practicing Stress Skills, you are teaching yourself how to proactively manage the emotional despair found in hopelessness and move toward positive feelings where you activate Hope.

What can get in the way of pausing for 90 seconds before reacting?

_____

_____

What can remind you to pause for 90 seconds instead of immediately reacting to the stress response in the future?

_____

_____

16 Bolte (2009)
17 Chu et al. (2024)

What kinds of situations make it hardest for you to pause before reacting?

_____

_____

How does your body typically feel in those moments when you want to react right away?

_____

_____

What thoughts or beliefs come up that make it feel urgent to act immediately?

_____

_____

Have there been times when you did pause before reacting? What helped you do that?

_____

_____

What tools (breathing, counting, grounding, etc.) could help you stay present during a 90-second pause?

_____

_____

Who in your life might support you in learning to pause and respond more calmly?

_____

_____

What could you say to yourself during a pause that would help you stay grounded and choose your next step thoughtfully?

_____

_____

STRESS SKILLS AND HORMONES

When we experience stress, our body releases elevated levels of cortisol, epinephrine, and norepinephrine[17]. These increased stress hormones can sometimes drive us toward engaging in unhealthy activities as an attempt to alleviate the stress. Such activities may include:

- Ignoring or denying stress
- Becoming isolated or withdrawn
- Using substances
- Procrastinating or avoiding responsibilities
- Talking negatively to self
- Self-harm
- Aggression or anger outbursts
- Neglecting one's health

ALLOSTATIC LOAD

We all experience stress, it's entirely normal. Experts believe we need a certain amount of stress to function at an optimum level because stress motivates us to make changes and reach our goals.

However, persistent stress leads to many negative consequences that can have a lasting effect on our overall health and well-being; this is called the allostatic load. We experience the allostatic load when the challenges we face in our environment exceed our ability to cope.

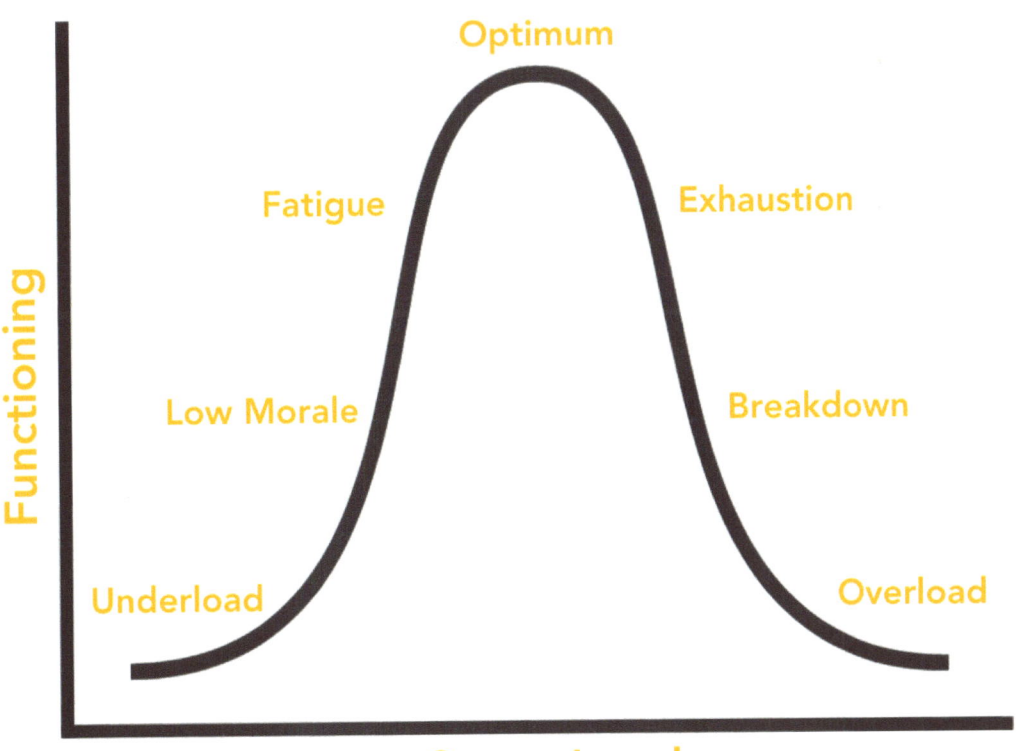

What are some other examples of unhealthy ways to manage stress?

Although these hormones are linked to our stress response, they are essential for helping us handle stress, maintain balance, and support daily functions, making it important to find healthy ways for their expression.

Hormone	Healthy Activation	Unhealthy Activation
Cortisol[18] • Helps the body cope with stress by increasing alertness and energy levels • Plays a role in memory and learning	• Exercise • Healthy nutrition • Outdoor activities	• Prolonged negatively charged emotions • Lack of sleep • Overexercising
Adrenaline (Epinephrine)[19] • Ignites the fight or flight response • Increases alertness, attention, and focus to help respond to stressful situations	• Roller coasters • Concerts • Confronting fears	• Violent behaviors • Excessive caffeine intake • Dangerous stunts
Norepinephrine[20] • Works with Adrenaline to ignite the fight or flight response • Bursts of this can lead to happiness	• Cold plunges • Goal setting • Practicing stress skills	• Intense anger or aggression • Self-harm • Over exerting the body

18 Cleveland Clinic (2021)

19 Cleveland Clinic (2022a)

20 Cleveland Clinic (2022b)

What happens if we have too much or too little of these hormones?

Hormone	Too Much	Too Little
Cortisol	Anxiety, depression, slower recovery from exercise, irritability	Fatigue, irritability, anxiety, depression
Adrenaline (Epinephrine)	Adverse health outcomes (i.e., irregular heartbeat and headaches)	Depression, lack of energy
Norepinephrine	High blood pressure, rapid or irregular heart beat, severe headache	Lack of concentration, depression, lethargy

When you use unhealthy ways to deal with stress, it may feel temporarily relieving because happy hormones like dopamine are released, which gives us a brief sense of pleasure or distraction. However, these coping mechanisms do not address the root causes of stress and can actually make things worse, keeping you in the downstairs brain.

Instead of resorting to unhealthy ways to manage stress, it's crucial to focus on developing healthy stress skills. These skills are like superpowers that help you handle your emotions after that initial 90-second stress response. They guide you toward using your "upstairs brain," which is responsible for clear thinking and making safe choices.

STRESS SKILLS: DEEP BREATHING ACTIVITY

One Stress Skill you can practice anywhere is deep belly breathing. Belly breathing differs from typical breathing because it encourages full oxygen exchange, meaning it allows the body to fully trade carbon dioxide with incoming oxygen[21]. Additionally, belly breathing slows the heart rate and lowers blood pressure, which are two physiological processes that are strained during increased stress.

21 Harvard Health Publishing (2016)

Today, try to intentionally practice deep belly breathing at least five times throughout the day, for at least 90 seconds each time. If you can, take deep breaths when you feel yourself sinking into your downstairs brain or you feel the stress response kicking in.

As you take your deep breaths, follow these steps:

- Sit in a comfortable position with your back as straight as possible.
- Notice how your body feels. Take a few seconds to just relax. Relax your neck, shoulders, arms, legs, and feet. Can you feel your heartbeat? Can you sense your breath? Try a few big inhales and exhales.
- When you're ready, place one hand on your chest and the other on your belly button (below the rib cage).
- Now take a long, slow, deep breath, in through your nose for a count of 10 (or as long as you are able). As you breathe in, you want to send the air to your belly button. Your hand on your belly should rise while the hand on your chest remains still.
- Once you get to 10, slowly exhale out of your mouth. Feel the muscles of your stomach tighten and your hand lower.
- Do this for at least 90 seconds (or 10 slow, deep breaths).

As you breathe, pay attention to how your brain and body feel before, during, and after the deep breathing.

How did you feel before taking the deep breaths? How did you feel after?

_____

_____

_____

_____

Make sure you use a stopwatch to time your breathing so you can experience the full 90-seconds. This is the amount of time it takes the stress hormones to cycle through your system after you experience a trigger.

STOP. *BREATHE.* RELAX.

Directions: Circle your top four favorite stress skills from the list below. If there are additional Stress Skills you use that are not on the list, use the space below to add them.

90 second pause	Sensory engagement	Laughter
Belly breathing	Cold plunge	Crying
Journaling	Decluttering	Tapping
Gardening	Prayer	Yoga
Calming music	Nature walk	Mantras

MY FAVORITE STRESS SKILLS

-
-
-
-
-
-
-
-
-

-
-
-
-
-
-
-
-
-

REFLECTION QUESTIONS

What are the signs that you are in your downstairs brain?

_____

_____

_____

_____

How does your stress impact your goals?

_____

_____

_____

_____

Why is managing stress important for Hope?

_____

_____

_____

_____

How is stress impacting your recovery?

_____

_____

_____

_____

How can you more positively manage your stress?

_____

_____

_____

_____

How can you notice when others are in their upstairs and downstairs brain?

_____

_____

_____

_____

How can you more proactively interact with them during those times?

_____

_____

_____

_____

How does not managing the 90-second pause impact my life?

_____

_____

_____

_____

What can I do during my 90-second pause?

_____

_____

_____

_____

Who can I practice the 90-second pause with?

_____

_____

_____

_____

MY SHINE HOPE STORY

Expanding on the "My Shine Hope Story" you began in the previous module (pg. 21), consider the Stress Skills you employed during a past challenge or could employ to ease the feelings of despair during the current challenge. How can Stress Skills help?

If you are writing about someone else, what Stress Skills did they use when faced with the challenge?

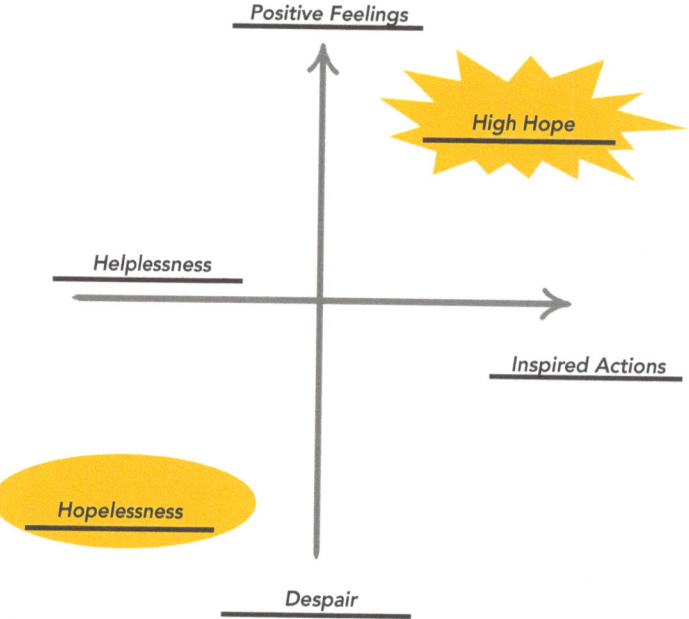

Hope Matrix Page 11

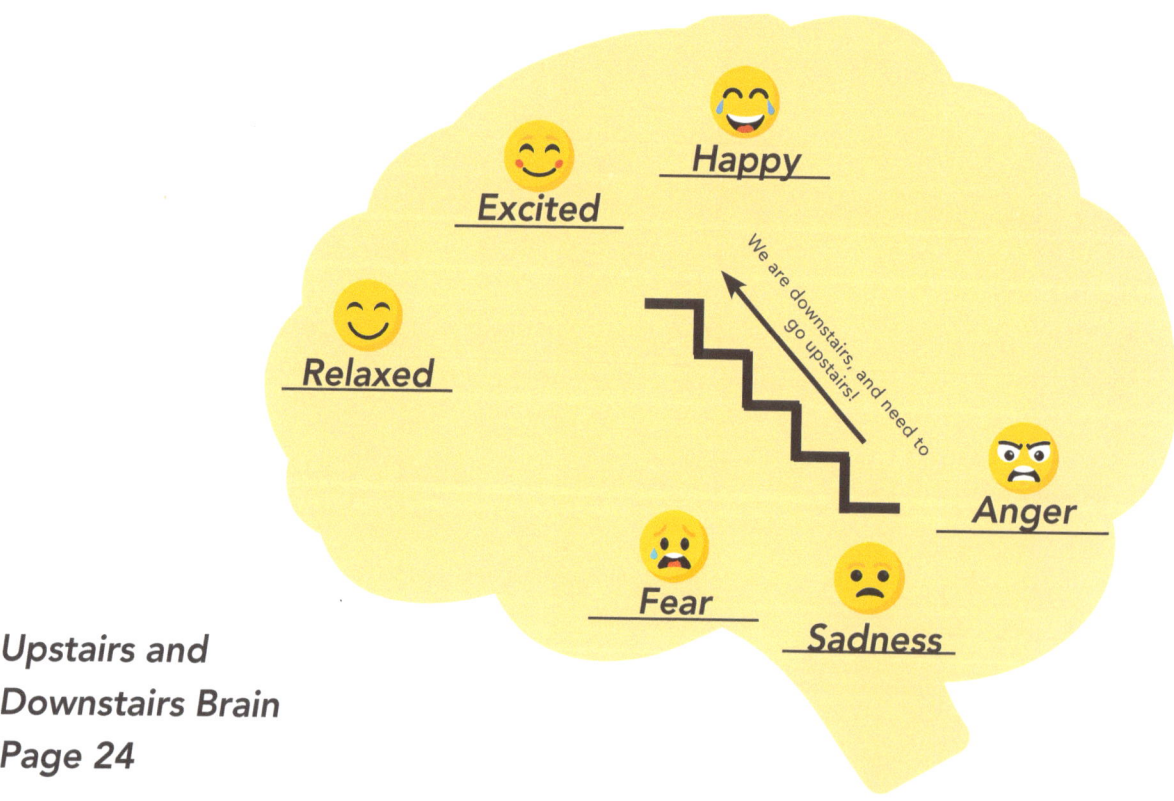

Upstairs and
Downstairs Brain
Page 24

MODULE 4:

HAPPINESS HABITS

HAPPINESS HABITS

The Second Key to Shine Hope is activating Hope using Happiness Habits[22].

Happiness Habits are healthy, long-term actions that cause your brain to release endorphins, dopamine, serotonin, and oxytocin. Happiness Habits help you stay in your upstairs brain, where you access the problem-solving skills, collaboration, and passion critical for Hope.

Like Stress Skills, different Happiness Habits work for different people. Therefore, it's important that you try numerous Happiness Habits to find the ones that most successfully help you stay in your upstairs brain.

Positive feelings are the feelings that help you maintain a hopeful mindset and encourage you to keep moving toward your goals. If you want to have a strong, hopeful mindset, you want to spend as much time as possible in your upstairs brain.

When you perform your Happiness Habits, your brain releases happiness hormones, including endorphins, dopamine, serotonin, and oxytocin. When these chemicals are released, you experience increased levels of happiness, which in turn fosters positive feelings. When you maintain daily Happiness Habits, you are ensuring future happiness and Hope.

Stress Skills	Positive Feelings	Happiness Habits
Help to quickly move from downstairs brain to upstairs brain; combats cortisol that's released in times of stress. • Used in times of stress • An Intervention when you feel stress • Can provide relief from the stress • **TIP: Remember the 90-second response**		Help keep in upstairs brain & your brain releases happiness hormones, including endorphins, dopamine, serotonin, and oxytocin. When these chemicals are released, you experience increased levels of happiness. • Used all the time • A prevention against stress • Can help maintain positive emotions • **TIP: Remember to practice Happiness Habits regularly**

22 Yaghobi & Khalilpoor (2022)
23 Saripalli (2022)

HAPPINESS HABITS AND HORMONES

Hormones related to happiness are dopamine, serotonin, and endorphins. Dopamine, serotonin, endorphins, and oxytocin—often called the "feel-good" hormones—play crucial roles in mood, motivation, and overall well-being[24]. However, there are both healthy and unhealthy ways to activate them. While healthy activation enhances mental health, unhealthy activation provides a quick hormonal boost but ultimately leads to dependency and mood instability.

Hormone	Healthy Activation	Unhealthy Activation
Dopamine[25] • Part of the reward system, or process in the brain that connects an event to a positive reward like happiness • Increases motivation and concentration	• Healthy diet • Creative activities • Protected sunlight exposure • Accomplishing goals	• Drug/alcohol use • Excessive social media use • Risky behaviors (i.e., reckless driving, harm to oneself)
Serotonin[26] • Helps with learning and memory • Helps regulate mood, making us feel emotionally stable, happier, and calmer	• Adequate sleep • Acts of kindness • Socializing • Expressing gratitude • Mindfulness	• Over-reliance on social media for validation • Overeating • Drug/alcohol use
Endorphin[27] • Help reduce stress by promoting relaxation • Plays a role in social bonding and connections • Acts as a natural painkiller and induces feelings of happiness and well-being	• Exercise • Hugs • Spending time in nature • Dancing	• Compulsive shopping • Violence • Risky sexual behaviors
Oxytocin[28] • Helps with social bonding and is linked to feelings of trust • Has a calming effect, reducing stress and anxiety levels • Linked to altruism and generosity	• Social interaction • Laughter • Pet interaction	• Risky sexual behaviors • Unhealthy relationships

When you perform your Happiness Habits, your brain releases happiness hormones, including endorphins, dopamine, serotonin, and oxytocin. When these chemicals are released, you experience increased levels of happiness, which in turn fosters positive feelings. When you maintain daily Happiness Habits, you are ensuring future happiness and Hope.

What happens if we have too much or too little of these hormones?

Hormone	Too Much	Too Little
Dopamine	Poor impulse control, increased aggression, and increased addiction	Increases in depression and anhedonia (i.e., loss of the ability to feel pleasure), and poor motivation
Serotonin	Increased agitation, restlessness, confusion	Depression and Hopelessness
Endorphin	Increased sleep disturbance and addiction	Increased depression and pain
Oxytocin	Difficulty bonding and connection, reduced empathy and trust, depression, and social anxiety	Overattachment, aggression, anxiety, gullibility

It is important to keep the happy hormones in balance with Happiness Habits. Just like stress hormones, we can have too much. So beware of how you feel, and be sure to notice if you are feeling off emotionally as it can often have an underlying cause. Be sure to ask your doctor for help if you need it.

24 Saripalli (2022)

25 Cleveland Clinic (2022c)

26 Cleveland Clinic (2022d)

27 Cleveland Clinic (2022e)

28 Cleveland Clinic (2022f)

Directions: Circle your top four favorite happiness habits from the list below. If there are additional happiness habits you use that are not on the list, use the space below to add them.

Activating purpose	Exercising / Nutrition	Volunteering
Pursuing passion	Creating / listening to music	Wonder / Awe
Utilizing strengths	Dancing / Singing	Quality sleep
Meditation	Drawing / Painting	Doodling
Smiling	Gratitude	

My Favorite Healthy Happiness Habits:

-
-
-
-

-
-
-

How can your spiritual practice help you practice happiness habits?

_____

_____

PRACTICING HAPPINESS HABITS

Take time to practice at least one new Happiness Habit each day this week. When life gets busy, it can be tempting to skip your Happiness Habits. However, it is important to practice Happiness Habits every day, especially when you are stressed. Happiness Habits combat the negative impact of stress hormones and help us maintain the Hopeful mindset we need to navigate challenging times.

What Happiness Habits did you practice this week?

1. _____

2. _____

3. _____

4. _____

5. _____

6. _____

7. _____

Which Happiness Habits did you enjoy the most? Why?

_____

_____

_____

_____

What Happiness Habits did you enjoy most as a kid? Are you doing them today?
Why or why not?

_____

_____

_____

_____

Think about one of the Happiness Habit you enjoyed the most, and answer the following questions:

How did your body feel before practicing your Happiness Habit?

_____

_____

How did your body feel during your Happiness Habit?

_____

_____

How did your body feel after practicing your Happiness Habit?

_____

_____

How did the Happiness Habit impact your thinking?

_____

_____

Was there a day that you didn't feel like you had time for a Happiness Habit? How did it feel
to make time for it anyway?

_____

_____

_____

_____

HAPPINESS HABITS: GRATITUDE

This exercise is an excerpt from Dr. Dan Tomasulo's book, "Learned Hopefulness."[29] Take five minutes to write down everything that happened yesterday. Pay attention to what happened, how it made you feel, and how you responded. Focus on your thoughts and feelings during your reflection.

Gratitude is one of the Happiness Habits that can help us stay in our upstairs brain. Take the next five minutes to once again write down everything that happened yesterday, but now, frame it through the lens of gratitude. What were you grateful for? When things didn't go as you wanted or you were triggered, what could you find to still be grateful for?

MY SHINE HOPE STORY

Expanding on the "My Shine Hope Story" you began in Module 2 (pg. 21), consider what Happiness Habits you need to practice to manage your current challenge or what Happiness Habits you practiced previously to overcome a past challenge. Think about the Happiness Habits that are non-negotiables for you and how your mood and thinking patterns change when you continue to practice the Happiness Habits.

If you are writing about someone else, what Happiness Habits did they use and how did it help them during their challenge?

29 Tomasulo (2020)

MODULE 5:

INSPIRED ACTIONS

INSPIRED ACTIONS

The Third Key to Shine Hope is taking Inspired Actions using a variety of goal-setting techniques.[30] Inspired Actions, the second ingredient of Hope, are the actions that we take as we move from hopelessness toward what we want in life. Inspired Actions specifically target motivational helplessness, the second ingredient of hopelessness, and move you toward what you are hopeful for in life.

How do we get out of helplessness? Through evidence-based approaches to goal setting. Our aim here is to teach you what we know about what makes you most likely to achieve all you want in life.

When we are struggling, it is important that we don't set too many goals or focus on too many things only to not achieve anything. If you are really down, sometimes focusing on just one goal, and making progress every day, is a step in the right direction. Add goals as you feel able to, and make sure you have someone to check in with regularly about your goals along the way.

GOAL SETTING WITH HOPE

Goal setting is an important part of the Hope Matrix. Even if we don't reach our goals, the simple act of setting the goal and working toward it can help us maintain a Hopeful Mindset. Don't let yourself lose Hope if you have to change or update your goals.

As we mentioned, our definition of Hope is a vision for something in the future, fueled by positive feelings and inspired actions. When we set goals for our future, it's important to set achievement goals, instead of avoidance goals. Achievement goals are created based on what we want to obtain, while avoidance goals are created based on things we don't want to happen. For example, if you are focused on fitness, set goals like "I will finish the marathon," rather than "I won't quit halfway through the marathon."

It is also important to set **intrinsic goals**, rather than extrinsic goals[32]. Extrinsic goals pertain to external achievements, such as wealth, power, or fame, and are associated with anxiety, depression, and lower happiness.

---

30 Yeasting & Jung (2010)

31 Urdan (2010)

32 Lee & Pounders (2019)

Intrinsic goals, on the other hand, are goals that pertain to your passions and core values, and are always focused on one of three things: meaningful relationships, personal growth, or community contributions. Intrinsic goals are positively associated with well-being, happiness, and high psychological health.

For example, if you are setting a goal for exercise, an intrinsic goal would be "I will exercise to feel healthier" rather than "I will exercise to impress others."

You can begin to brainstorm goals using the **WOOP Framework**[33]. The WOOP Framework includes four steps: **W**(wish), **O**(outcome), **O**(obstacle), and **P**(plan):

WISH: Think about what you want in life. Pick a wish that is challenging but that you can still fulfill.

OUTCOME: What would be the best possible outcome if your wish came true? How would fulfilling your wish make you feel?

OBSTACLE: What is within you or in your environment that keeps you from fulfilling your wish?

PLAN: Identify one action you can take or thought you can think to overcome your obstacle. Then, make an if-then plan: IF (I encounter this obstacle) THEN (I will use this solution).

When setting goals, you want to ensure that you are setting **SMART Goals**: Goals that are Specific, Measurable, Attainable, Relevant, and Time-bound[34]. Refer to the SMART Goals poster for more information.

You should always have at least a few **stretch goals** for yourself. Stretch goals are long-term goals that you set to reach your purpose; they should stretch and challenge you, and inspire you to keep moving forward. It is good to have some stretch goals that help you go further than you might with SMART goals - as they can help us reach for more than we ever thought was possible.

For each stretch goal, you want to create **micro-goals.** Micro-goals are the small, achievable goals that help you move toward your stretch goals. They are the steps in the stepping process that help you continue looking toward the future. And remember- even your micro-goals should be achievement and intrinsic goals, not avoidance and extrinsic goals.

33 Saddawi-Konefka et al. (2017)

34 Lawlor, K (2012)

S.M.A.R.T. Goals

Specific
Be specific about your goal. Think about these questions when creating your goal: What needs to be accomplished? Who is responsible for it? What steps will you take to achieve it?

Measurable
Can you measure your progress? If this goal will take a long time to achieve, set shorter term goals to reach along the way.

Achievable
Are you inspired and motivated to reach your goal? Do you have the tools or skills you need? If not, do you know how you can get them?

Relevant
Does your goal go along with what you are trying to achieve in the future? Is it important to you? Is it something you care about?

Time-bound
Is your timing realistic? Can you achieve your goal in the time period set? Think about what you may want to achieve at the halfway point.

SETTING SMART GOALS USING WOOP

Practice goal-setting with the following prompts. A worksheet for you to use with future goals can be found on page 55.

Pick one area of your life (job, health, spiritual practice, relationships, etc.).
Brainstorm a goal using WOOP:

WISH   _____

OUTCOME   _____

OBSTACLE   _____

PLAN   _____

Based on your WOOP brainstorm, write down a stretch goal on the next page. Check all of the boxes that apply to your goal, then explain how your goal meets each of the criteria. If it doesn't meet one of the criteria, revise your goal and try again.

GOAL:

_____

_____

_____

_____

IS IT:	HOW?
SPECIFIC	_____
MEASURABLE	_____
ACHIEVABLE	_____
RELEVANT	_____
TIME-BOUND	_____

Is your goal an achievement goal?   YES   NO

Is your goal an intrinsic goal?   YES   NO

Now, use the stepping method to come up with five microgoals that will help you reach your goal

1 _____

2 _____

3 _____

4 _____

5 _____

What is a stretch goal you would like to work toward?

_____

_____

_____

_____

REFLECTION

What makes this goal important to you?

_____

_____

_____

_____

How can your strengths help you pick and set goals?

_____

_____

_____

_____

What strengths can you rely on to overcome obstacles?

_____

_____

_____

_____

How can spiritual practice help you as you work toward your goals?

_____

_____

_____

_____

What other areas of your life might you want to set goals for?

_____

_____

_____

_____

What are some goals you could set for those other areas of life?

_____

_____

_____

_____

Who can help support you as you work toward your goal(s)?

_____

_____

_____

_____

MY SHINE HOPE STORY

Building on the "My Shine Hope Story" from Module 1 (pg. 21), think about the goals you can set to overcome your current challenge or the goals you set when overcoming a past challenge. Break these goals down into smaller, manageable steps, and anticipate potential obstacles along with strategies to overcome them.

If you are writing about someone else, what goals did they set to overcome their challenge? How did they work to take steps toward reaching those goals? What obstacles did they face and how did they overcome those obstacles?

GOAL SETTING

Use this worksheet regularly in your goal setting process. Feel free to copy and complete for multiple goals, including family, relationships, health, and community. And remember to set some stretch goals, which takes you beyond the SMART process.

MY SMART GOAL: ⬭

IS IT:

SPECIFIC   **M**EASURABLE   **A**CHIEVABLE   **R**ELEVANT   **T**IME-BOUND

NO, IT'S A STRETCH GOAL! :)

Is your goal an achievement goal?	YES	NO	Is your goal an intrinsic goal?	YES	NO

What are the feelings associated with achieving this goal?

_____

_____

_____

Why do you want to achieve this goal?

_____

_____

_____

What positive affirmation am I willing to say daily to achieve this goal?

_____

_____

_____

To support this goal, I commit to regular practice of:

Three Stress Skills

_____

_____

_____

Three Happiness Habits

_____

_____

_____

Eliminating These Challenges

_____

_____

_____

What are six steps or microgoals that will help me reach my SMART goal?

1 _____ 3 _____ 5 _____

2 _____ 4 _____ 6 _____

Name 3 obstacles toward my SMART goals:

1 _____

2 _____

3 _____

Name multiple ways to overcome each obstacle:

_____

_____

_____

Name one person I can check in with regularly on this goal:

_____

What step can I take in the next five minutes to get closer to my goal.

_____

_____

_____

Contact this person now and make a regular appointment to check in: **DONE!**

MODULE 6:

NOURISHING NETWORKS

MODULE 6: NOURISHING NETWORKS

The Fourth Key to Shine Hope is creating and cultivating strong Nourishing Networks.[35] Your Nourishing Networks, also known as your Hope Networks, are the people in your life that provide you with support, help you stay on track, encourage you to succeed, and who you do the same for in return. You are up to 95% more likely to achieve a goal if you write it down and check in with someone regularly. Therefore, Nourishing Networks are critical support systems for moving you toward what you want in life.

Begin to brainstorm the people who belong in your Hope Networks and where they fit:

Friends and Family I count on:

_____

_____

People I turn to for Stress Skills:

_____

_____

People I practice Happiness Habits with:

_____

_____

Spiritual connections I practice:

_____

_____

Medical experts I can turn to when I need help:

_____

_____

Community resources I can utilize:

_____

_____

Where can I go in times of crisis?
ex. If you can't list anyone, you can check out our list of resources for how to get connected.
www.theshinehopecompany.com/recovery-resources/

_____

_____

35 Bunston et al. (1995)

STRENGTHENING YOUR HOPE NETWORK

Now that you've identified some of the people in your Hope Networks, how can you strengthen those relationships? You can enhance your Hope Networks using vulnerability, praise, recognition, kindness, gratitude, empathy, compassion, collaboration, strong communication, and the 5:1 rule.

The 5:1 rule states that for every one negative or constructive criticism you say to someone, you should say five positive things[36]. Pick one person from your Hope Networks and write down five things you love about them. Once you've written down all five, call or text the person you chose and tell them all five things.

1 _____

2 _____

3 _____

4 _____

5 _____

Who is one person I can go to in a time of need?

How can a support network help me in my recovery journey?

_____

_____

_____

_____

Remember, the size of your Hope Network doesn't matter, the quality of your connections matters. **The best way to receive support is to give support.**

MY SHINE HOPE STORY

Building on the "My Shine Hope Story" from module 1 (pg. 21), think about who you can turn to for help with your current challenge, or who you relied on in the past when overcoming a challenge. Who is the one person you can go to in times of crisis?

If you are writing about someone else, who is in their Nourishing Network? How did their Nourishing Network help them during the challenge?

36 Travers (2024)

MODULE 7:

ELIMINATING CHALLENGES

MODULE 7: ELIMINATING CHALLENGES

CHALLENGES TO HOPE

The Fifth Key to Shine Hope is Eliminating the Challenges[37]. Challenges to Hope are negative habits or thoughts that quickly take you to hopelessness, such as emotional despair and a sense of helplessness. The thought patterns are often unconscious habits we don't realize we're doing, so becoming aware of these patterns is critical. Once we know what they are and recognize them, it is important to counteract them so that we don't let them keep us from all we Hope for in life.

CHALLENGE #1: LIMITING BELIEFS Limiting beliefs are negative thoughts or opinions that we tell ourselves are true that keep us in a negative mindset. They are at the core of our anxieties, fears, and insecurities. In order to truly create, maintain, and grow Hope, we must first identify the limiting beliefs we have around Hope and find ways to overcome them.

CHALLENGE #2: AUTOMATIC NEGATIVE THOUGHTS (ANTs) Automatic negative thoughts (ANTs) are repetitive negative thoughts that we form instantaneously in response to external stimuli. They're often hurtful or irrational, and can send us into a spiral of hopelessness if not managed.

CHALLENGE #3: ALL-OR-NOTHING THINKING All-or-nothing thinking is a negative thought pattern in which we only think in extremes. Rather than seeing all of the solutions to a problem, all-or-nothing thinking forces us to only see either complete success or complete failure.

CHALLENGE #4: NEGATIVE BIAS Negativity bias refers to the psychological phenomenon that causes negative events to have a greater impact on our brains than positive ones. We tend to fixate on a criticism rather than a compliment, pay more attention to bad news than good news, and notice negative events happening near us instead of positive ones. Negativity bias forces us into our downstairs brain, and can have lasting impacts on our relationships, behavior, and Hope.

CHALLENGE #5: RUMINATION Rumination refers to when we repeatedly go over a thought or a problem from the past in our heads, without end. Rumination is associated with numerous negative mental states, including depression, anxiety, post-traumatic stress disorder, and hopelessness.

CHALLENGE #6: WORRY Worry is when we feel anxious or afraid about real or imagined future scenarios. Where rumination focuses on the past, worry focuses on the future. Worry forces us to fixate on and respond to future danger that we think we may encounter.

CHALLENGE #7: FOCUSING ON UNCONTROLLABLES Focusing on Uncontrollables is when you focus on things that are outside of your influence of power. This can lead to rumination and worry, which in turn can cause stress, anxiety, and depression. It is important to proactively manage what you can control and learn to release the rest.

CHALLENGE #8: ATTACHING TO OUTCOMES Attaching to outcomes is when we set goals, and are then unable or unwilling to be satisfied unless we reach that specific goal. While goal setting is important, it is also important to have a sense of active surrender and know that sometimes there is a better path. Being too attached to specific goal attainment leads to hopelessness when we don't reach that goal.

CHALLENGE #9: INTERNALIZING FAILURE There is actually a biological link between failure and our physical and mental health. When we achieve our goals, our brains release testosterone and dopamine, and we experience positive feelings. Science has found that, with time and repetition, these chemicals can alter the chemistry of our brains in positive ways.

The opposite is also true. If we fail early while others succeed, we are more likely to make future mistakes if, instead of learning from the failure, we let it affect our feeling state and future confidence.

To overcome this biological response and hopelessness cycle, the key is to learn how to avoid internalizing failure. Failure is an indication that one of the steps in your process failed, not that you failed. Once you learn to deconstruct the process and separate your identity from your process, you can end failure.

How can Stress Skills help you overcome negative thinking patterns?

_____

_____

How can your Hope network help you overcome negative thinking patterns?

_____

_____

ELIMINATING CHALLENGES PRACTICE: FOCUSING ON THE CONTROLLABLES

Inside the sunflower below, write down the things you can control. In the areas outside of the sunflower, write down the things you cannot control. This visual can be a reminder to focus on things inside the sunflower and find ways to release the stress and worry associated with the things outside of the sunflower.

THINGS THAT I CAN CONTROL

THINGS THAT I CANNOT CONTROL

WORKSHEET

Complete the statements below with your personal strategies for overcoming the challenges discussed in this lesson. For more ideas on how to overcome challenges, see an example of the completed worksheet on the next page.

When I'm experiencing Limiting Beliefs, my strategy to overcome this challenge is to

_____

_____

When I'm experiencing Automatic Negative Thoughts, my strategy to overcome this challenge is to

_____

_____

When I'm experiencing All-or-Nothing thinking, my strategy to overcome this challenge is to

_____

_____

When I experience Negative Bias, my strategy to overcome this challenge is to

_____

_____

When I experience Rumination, my strategy to overcome this challenge is to

_____

_____

When I experience Attachment to Outcomes, my strategy to overcome this challenge is to

_____

_____

When I experience Internalizing Failure, my strategy to overcome this challenge is to

_____

_____

Examples

When I'm experiencing Limiting Beliefs, my strategy to overcome this challenge is to
Remember my purpose and think through the evidence.

When I'm experiencing Automatic Negative Thoughts, my strategy to overcome this challenge is to:
Practice stress skills and think through the evidence.

When I'm experiencing All-or-Nothing thinking, my strategy to overcome this challenge is to: *Practice dialectical thinking.*

When I experience Negative Bias, my strategy to overcome this challenge is to
Practice my happiness habits.

When I experience Rumination, my strategy to overcome this challenge is to
Practice my stress skills.

When I experience Attachment to Outcomes, my strategy to overcome this challenge is to
Practice dialectical thinking.

When I experience Internalizing Failure, my strategy to overcome this challenge is to
Think through the evidence and remember my purpose

Working to Eliminate Challenges can be overwhelming sometimes. Where are places you feel safe and can go to when you're feeling overwhelmed?

_____

_____

MY SHINE HOPE STORY

Building on the "My Shine Hope Story" from Module 1 (pg. 21), think about the thinking patterns that might most impact your ability to move forward toward Hope. How can you overcome these patterns using the skills you've learned? If you're writing about a challenge you previously overcame, reflect on the thinking patterns you encountered and how you dealt with them. Would you address them differently now?

If you are writing about another person, what thinking patterns came up that impacted their ability to move forward toward Hope? How did they eliminate challenges?

BUILDING A VISION FOR HOPE

MEASURING YOUR HOPE

Now that you have reached the end of the course, take a moment to retake the Snyder Hope Scale to find your new Hope Score.

Use the link provided to take the Snyder Hope Scale Assessment:

www.theshinehopecompany.com/adult-hope-scale/

My initial Snyder Hope Scale Score: _____ /64

My Current Snyder Hope Scale Score: _____ /64

Did your score increase or decrease?

_____

_____

What positively or negatively impacted your score?

_____

_____

Remember, your Hope score will rise and fall as you go throughout your life. The score is simply a way for you to check in with yourself and keep yourself centered and focused on your Hope journey. The lower your score, the more you want to strengthen your Hope muscles using the Shine Hope framework.

Hope is a lifelong journey. Take time to think about where you want your journey to go now that the course is coming to an end.

What Hope skills will you practice to continue to create, maintain, and grow Hope in your life?

_____

_____

How will you inspire Hope in the lives of those around you?

_____

_____

How will Hope help you on your recovery journey?

_____

_____

ACTIVATING HOPE

The best way to improve and inspire your own Hope is to activate it in your life and your community. When you engage in volunteering activities, it not only benefits others but also has a positive impact on yourself. People who have volunteered often share that it boosts their self-confidence, self-esteem, and even brings them good luck.

According to a survey conducted on individuals who volunteered in the past year, an impressive 76% reported feeling physically better, a whopping 94% said that volunteering improved their mood, and 78% experienced reduced stress levels. So, by lending a hand to others, you not only make a difference but also enhance your own well-being and hopefulness.

Here are 7 ways that you can cultivate Hope in the people around you:

Teach Hope: Remember, we are not born with Hope, it is a skill we must be taught and many individuals just like yourself are living life without these skills, so share this course with your colleague, organization, place of worship, or anywhere else you find community. You can also start teaching your peers how to Hope. You can explore the Hopeful Mindsets curriculums today, by visiting www.theshinehopecompany.com/shine-Hope/

Hang Posters for Hope: Put up posters so that others can find the science of Hope and start activating it in their own lives. Get your Shine Hope Posters at www.theshinehopecompany.com/shine-Hope/

Create a Hope Initiative at your Organization: How can your organization more successfully help people in recovery move from hopelessness to Hope? Starting a Shine Hope Club or implementing the Five Day Global Hope Challenge are great ways to influence positive changes in your organization. Learn more at **www.theshinehopecompany.com/shine-Hope/**

Put up Yard Signs for Hope: Yard Signs can be placed in your yard or your window to share the message of 'how' to Hope with your community, as they have QR codes directing people to the no cost resources like the five day challenge and Hope scales. The purpose of the sign is to spread the message of the power of Hope and encourage people to start learning about Hope and using Hope tools. Our yard signs are no cost to download and print yourself or are available for purchase in our store:
Check out our Yard Signs at: **www.theshinehopestore.com/products/yard-signs**

Plant a Sunflower Garden for Hope: We use the sunflower as the global symbol for Hope, and grow them all over the world. The sunflower is used to create universal symbolism and "brand" for Hope. The power of a brand is transformative, as repeated messaging helps reinforce the primary message that Hope is positive, a skill that must be learned, and moves us from darkness to light.

Our garden signs are free to download and print yourself or are available for purchase in our store. They have QR codes directing people to the free resources like the five day challenge and Hope scales on our website. We encourage you to plant a garden in your yard, in a pot on your windowsill (there are small sunflower species), or start a community garden of sunflowers. Hope is always better when shared. Find out more here
www.theshinehopecompany.com/gardening

Get Support: Everyone needs help managing stress, and it is so important to be proactive about your Hope. It is also important to be open with others, so they feel OK about getting help. Check out the resources available at:
www.theshinehopecompany.com/Hope-science/general/

Activate your City: Reach out to your major or public officials to activate Hope throughout your entire city. Our Hopeful Cities Playbook provides the blueprint for activating Hope across numerous major sectors within a city.
Find out more information at **www.Hopefulcities.org**

GROUP ACTIVITY
MAKE A PLAN TO SPREAD HOPE

Discuss and make a plan for how your group can teach others about Hope.

Who will your group reach out to about Hope skills?

_____

_____

When will your group reach out to the individual(s)/organization?

_____

_____

What will your group say to them to convince them that Hope is important?

_____

_____

How will your group facilitate teaching Hope to them?

_____

_____

We would also love your feedback on the My Shine Hope Story course as we continue to improve and revise based on feedback and research. Please take a few moments to complete the Post-Course Survey.

https://form.jotform.com/251113275074449

SHINE HOPE™
A HOW-TO FOR HOPE IN TRYING TIMES

Scan to download the clickable version of this infographic

STRESS SKILLS	**H**APPINESS HABITS	**I**NSPIRED ACTIONS	**N**OURISHING NETWORKS	**E**LIMINATING CHALLENGES
90 second pause	Activating purpose	WOOP process	5:1 Rule	Limiting beliefs
Belly breathing	Pursuing passion	SMART goals	Compassion	Automatic Negative Thoughts (ANTs)
Journaling	Utilizing strengths	Stretch goals	Forgiveness	All-or-nothing thinking
Gardening	Meditation	Achievement goals	Love	Negative bias
Calming music	Smiling	Intrinsic goals	Gratitude	Rumination & Worry
Affirming beliefs	Exercising / Nutrition	Mastery goals	Recognition	Focusing on Uncontrollables
Sensory engagement	Creating / listening to music	Micro goals / Stepping	Support	Attaching to outcomes
Cold plunge	Dancing / Singing	Habit Stacking	Faith	Internalizing failure
Decluttering	Drawing / Painting	Visualization	Trust	Toxic Consumption
Prayer	Gratitude	Overcoming obstacles	Respect	Nocebo Effect
Nature walk	Volunteering	Regoaling	Effective Listening	Mind Wandering
Napping	Wonder / Awe	Write down goals / check in	Empathy	Implicit Bias
Laughter	Quality sleep		Kindness	Negative Framing
Crying	Doodling		Animals	Perfectionism
Tapping				Taking things personally
Yoga				
Mantras				

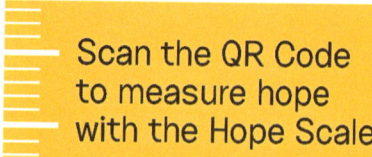
Scan the QR Code to measure hope with the Hope Scale!

STRESS SKILLS

Stress Skills are actions that help you navigate your stress response and work through your body's chemical response to external stimuli. By practicing them, you are teaching yourself how to proactively manage the emotional despair found in hopelessness and move towards positive feelings where you activate hope.

The Stress Response

This is when you are emotionally triggered by something in your environment, and you go into fight, flight, freeze, or fawn mode as your body releases stress hormones, such as cortisol, adrenaline, and norepinephrine. You are in your downstairs brain, and can't reach your upstairs brain; the upstairs brain is the place where you make good decisions for moving towards all you hope for in life.

90 second pause	Sensory engagement	Laughter
Belly breathing	Cold plunge	Crying
Journaling	Decluttering	Tapping
Gardening	Prayer	Yoga
Calming music	Nature walk	Mantras
Affirming beliefs	Napping	

HAPPINESS HABITS

Happiness Habits are healthy, long-term actions that cause your brain to release happiness hormones including endorphins, dopamine, serotonin, and oxytocin. Happiness Habits help you stay in your upstairs brain, where you access the problem-solving skills, collaboration, and passion critical for hope.

Positive Feelings

Positive feelings, the first ingredient of hope, are feelings that are located in your upstairs brain like wonder, joy, and peace that make it easier to overcome obstacles that get in the way of hope. You proactively manage the emotional despair of hopelessness using Stress Skills and use your Happiness Habits to stay in your upstairs brain, where you then energetically move towards your goals in life.

Activating purpose	Exercising / Nutrition	Volunteering
Pursuing passion	Creating / listening to music	Wonder / Awe
Utilizing strengths	Dancing / Singing	Quality sleep
Meditation	Drawing / Painting	Doodling
Smiling	Gratitude	

INSPIRED ACTIONS

Inspired Actions, the second ingredient of hope, are the deliberate steps you take toward your goals in life. Inspired Actions help you to move away from the motivational helplessness, the second ingredient of hopelessness, and toward what you are hopeful for in life.

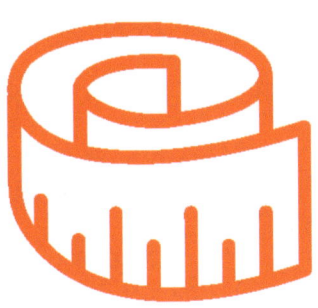

Types of Goals:

WOOP

Achievement

Intrinsic

SMART

Stretch

Micro-Goals

Pathways, Agency, and Regoaling

Obstacles are inevitable, and sometimes you can't reach the goal as you intended. It is important to embrace obstacles to goals, learn to pivot or reevaluate, be flexible and adaptable, and never be afraid to ask for help.

If a goal seems too big, use the stepping process or create micro-goals to chunk it down into smaller goals. Think of one thing you can do in the next 20 minutes. And know when you need to re-goal.

NOURISHING NETWORKS

Your Nourishing Networks, also known as your Hope Networks, are the people in your life that provide you with support, help you stay on track, encourage you to succeed, and who you do the same for in return. You are up to 95% more likely to achieve a goal if you write it down, and check in with someone regularly. So Nourishing Networks are critical support systems for moving you towards what you hope for in life.

Your Hope Networks should include:

People who know and understand you.

People who value your strengths.

People who activate the SHINE framework.

People whom you trust and can confide in.

People who are available to support you.

People you are willing to do the above for as well.

Enhancing Your Hope Networks

Enhance your Hope Networks using the 5:1 rule, vulnerability, praise, recognition, kindness, gratitude, empathy, compassion, collaboration, and strong communication, and be sure to have different networks for different areas of life.

Don't forget to include doctors, therapists, and/or other medical professionals in your Hope Networks.

ELIMINATING CHALLENGES

Challenges to Hope are negative habits of thought that quickly take you to hopelessness, that emotional despair and sense of helplessness. The thought patterns are often unconscious habits, so becoming aware of these patterns is critical. Once we know what they are and recognize them, it is important to counteract them so that we don't let them keep us from all we hope for in life.

Eliminating Challenges

Most of the Challenges to Hope take constant, repetitive actions to change and overcome. Thanks to the science of neuroplasticity, we know it is possible with practice and dedication. The key is to learn to identify what specific challenges happen most frequently and then proactively find ways to manage those challenges.

Limiting beliefs	Focusing on Uncontrollables	Mind Wandering
Automatic Negative Thoughts (ANTs)	Attaching to outcomes	Implicit Bias
All-or-nothing thinking		Negative Framing
	Internalizing failure	Perfectionism
Negative bias	Toxic Consumption	
Rumination & Worry	Nocebo Effect	Taking things personally